SHARING JESUS WITH CONFIDENCE

How to Be a Gospeler and Have

Conversations That Matter for Eternity

WILLIE ROBERTSON

A GOSPELER RESOURCE

W PUBLISHING GROUP

AN IMPRINT OF THOMAS NELSON

ISBN 978-1-4003-3851-1 (booklet)
ISBN 978-1-4003-3852-8 (ePub)

Library of Congress Control Number: 2023941253

Printed in the United States of America
24 25 26 27 28 LBC 5 4 3 2 1

CONTENTS

Introduction vii

1. CONFIDENCE TO SHARE 1
Imitating Jesus 1
Gearing Up 7

2. CONFIDENCE TO START 12
The Starting Point 12
Learning Someone's Story 13

3. CONFIDENCE TO CHALLENGE 18
Faith in Relationships 18
Faith in the Unseen 21
Belief in God's Word 22

4. CONFIDENCE IN CHRIST 23

Believing in the Savior 23

Forgiveness 26

Commitment to Jesus 28

5. CONFIDENCE IN THE PROCESS 30

Choosing a Side 30

The Holy Spirit 32

Repentance 35

Baptism 37

New Spirit-Led Life 39

Light vs. Darkness 41

6. CONFIDENCE IN THE COMMISSION 44

Telling Others Jesus Is Lord of Your Life 44

Becoming a Gospeler 47

Sharing Jesus with Confidence Quick Guide 50

My Challenge to You 53

About the Author 55

Worship Christ as Lord of your life.
And if someone asks about your hope as
a believer, always be ready to explain it.

1 PETER 3:15 NLT

INTRODUCTION

IF YOU ARE A BELIEVER AND A FOLLOWER OF JESUS CHRIST, I am so glad you have taken another step of faith to learn to share what should be not only an important part of your life but the very foundation of your hope. I trust this resource will give you the insight and knowledge you need to be bold in your conversations with anyone who may be searching spiritually as you talk to them about a journey with Jesus. There isn't only one way or perfect method of sharing your faith, but if you have often wondered where to start, I believe what I am about to guide you through should help.

I find in most or in almost all areas of my life where I am confident, there are two qualities present: knowledge and experience. Once I have a good grasp on something—a fair amount of understanding on a subject—experience just adds to my confidence. Of course, that doesn't always mean I do things perfectly, but these two advantages are a must for me to even attempt most anything.

For you to get to the place where you feel like you could share Jesus with anyone, I want to help you excel in both knowledge and experience. I know that learning how to do anything better, or even just how to get started, can be a real challenge. Trust me when I say that it will all be worth the effort once you see someone's life changed because of Jesus and you know your obedience to Him sparked the conversation for faith to begin.

Whether someone shared Jesus with you this year, thirty years ago, or anywhere in between, I'm going to share some Bible verses that are not only beneficial when sharing your faith with someone but are pivotal for your own faith in Jesus too. My prayer is that this booklet will be a tool for you to lay a strong foundation so you can share Jesus with others as the Spirit leads you.

You can be knowledgeable. You can be bold. You can be prepared to be a light in darkness.

Be Jesus!

Chapter 1

CONFIDENCE TO SHARE

IMITATING JESUS

Motivation is crucial in helping us accomplish just about anything we set our minds on. But motivation without direction often keeps us from taking the first step. Imitation is not just a form of flattery but is the way so many big ideas get accomplished. When we see others do something great, we try to do what they did. When it comes to a relationship with Jesus, it's no different. In fact, the Bible tells us, "In your relationships with one another, have the same mindset as Christ Jesus" (Philippians 2:5). Following Jesus becomes more than words—it's how we live out our faith every day.

We know that we have come to know him if we keep his commands. Whoever says, "I know him," but does not do what he commands is a liar, and the truth is not in that person. But if anyone obeys his word, love for God is truly made complete in them. This is how we know we are in him: Whoever claims to live in him must live as Jesus did. (1 John 2:3–6)

If we are supposed to live like Jesus lived, then how exactly did He live?

He wasn't just a nice person and a great neighbor who tried to get to church services as often as He could. What stands out to me is how He pleased His Father and cared so deeply for people. He was especially keen to those who were lost and lacked belief in anything beyond what they could see on this earth.

Jesus has a heart for the lost, so to live like Him, we must have that same heart.

"For the Son of Man came to seek and to save the lost." (Luke 19:10)

In the verse above Jesus states His mission of saving people who are lost, revealing the Father's plan for why He came here.

"For God did not send his Son into the world to condemn the world, but to save the world through him." (John 3:17)

"Seek and save" is such an interesting phrase and involves proactively moving toward lost people. From my experience it's never been difficult to find those who are lost around me, but seeking them for the Lord goes much further than simply seeing them. The only One who can save is Jesus, but He is also seeking. When our motivation becomes salvation for the lost like Jesus' was when He was here, we start seeking their hearts and souls for Christ. So the question becomes: how aggressively do we seek?

Think about when you seek out a good TV show to watch or a pair of jeans that fit you just right. How do you approach seeking something of this nature? Is there any urgency? Do you make a plan? Most likely it's fairly casual. You're looking, but it's not earth-shattering.

Now, think about seeking your lost car keys or your wallet or your purse. This is where seeking becomes our number one priority. Everything else stops when we seek these items because, for most of us, life stops for us when we don't have them. I have often misplaced and outright lost both my wallet and car keys. Without cash or credit cards, you lose access to buying anything. Without your driver's license and your keys, you can't drive. You. Are. Stuck.

I know some of you are saying, "But Willie, that's why I have *everything* on my phone. I can start my car, buy anything, and do pretty much everything I want on there." For you, when that phone is misplaced or lost, life shuts down. And I'd say most freak out more about that than losing anything else. You've lost your contacts, your pictures, your access to social media accounts, and your schedule. The list goes on and on.

These days seeking a lost phone becomes a mission! You have a sense of urgency because you can't imagine going through your day without it. You'll work back through every move you made with every detail being critical. Most of the tools to help you find it were on the phone too. You usually need to seek people to help you find it, but of course you can't call them. And you likely have never memorized their actual phone numbers. So you have to literally seek them too.

When you really want something to be found, you reach the point where you must take action and seek. Are we as concerned with seeking lost people for the Gospel? When Jesus states that He came to seek and save the lost, He had just done that very thing when He ran into a guy named Zaccheus. Here's their conversation.

4

Jesus entered Jericho and was passing through. A man was there by the name of Zacchaeus; he was a chief tax collector and was wealthy. He wanted to see who Jesus was, but because he was short he could not see over the crowd. So he ran ahead and climbed a sycamore-fig tree to see him, since Jesus was coming that way.

When Jesus reached the spot, he looked up and said to him, "Zacchaeus, come down immediately. I must stay at your house today." So he came down at once and welcomed him gladly.

All the people saw this and began to mutter, "He has gone to be the guest of a sinner."

But Zacchaeus stood up and said to the Lord, "Look, Lord! Here and now I give half of my possessions to the poor, and if I have cheated anybody out of anything, I will pay back four times the amount."

Jesus said to him, "Today salvation has come to this house, because this man, too, is a son of Abraham. For the Son of Man came to seek and to save the lost." (Luke 19:1–10)

This is a great example of what seeking means and how seeking looks. The first thing I notice is how Jesus cared enough to actually engage Zacchaeus in a conversation. Not swayed at all by what the crowd thought, Jesus showed this wealthy tax collector that his life had meaning. But then Jesus took even more action and went to his home for a visit. His mission was on full display by how He treated this one person who was despised by most everyone.

Our lives will be filled with similar stories of these types of conversations when we decide to walk with Jesus on His seek-and-save mission. If you read my book *Gospeler*, you read that that's what happened when my aunt's pastor went to a bar in another state to share the Gospel with my dad.

As stated earlier, we can find lost people all around us, because they aren't exactly hiding. But truly seeking them to help them find their way to salvation? Now *that* is the difficult part. Jesus left this earth after giving all His followers the instructions to do this very thing. He gave a final directive to those who had spent the last few years with Him.

> Then Jesus came to them and said, "All author-
> ity in heaven and on earth has been given to me.
> Therefore go and make disciples of all nations, bap-
> tizing them in the name of the Father and of the
> Son and of the Holy Spirit, and teaching them to
> obey everything I have commanded you. And surely

I am with you always, to the very end of the age."
(Matthew 28:18–20)

Today my hope is that the Church—the body of Christ—will reengage with His words and take on His mission to seek and save the lost as we live out what He commissioned us to do. We can't do this casually, like we're just shopping, but intentionally, more like looking for a lost phone.

My prayer is that you can become confident in sharing your faith after reading my challenge to you. My next hope is that sharing Jesus becomes the mission that defines you as a person. There are countless lost people out there, so let's go! Let's start seeking and telling them the story of Jesus Christ, the only One who can save them!

> Instead, you must worship Christ as Lord of your life.
> And if someone asks about your hope as a believer,
> always be ready to explain it. (1 Peter 3:15 NLT)

GEARING UP

It's amazing how far we will go to try to prepare for all that life throws at us. In fact, much of our lives is based on training and preparation. We spend years in school to be prepared to make a living. Many then go on to higher education to learn more to prepare for a specific career. Most formal education involves taking tests where you are expected to explain and prove what you've learned.

Since our family's TV show *Duck Dynasty* ended, I spend a lot of time traveling to speak at events, and I pride myself on my preparation for any trip I take. While experience makes attention to details second nature, we all get thrown curveballs from time to time, no matter how prepared we feel. There are flight delays, cancellations, missed connections, car rental challenges, and problems with reservations. That's just the nature of travel.

For anything we do in life, experience builds memory to make the next time easier. But when we get derailed by something or someone we never saw coming, that's when another key principle must kick in: patience. Problems are going to happen, so when we prepare for them, patience helps put them in the category of gaining more experience.

Because I fly so much, it's easy to spot the folks at any airport who have not properly prepared or obviously have little experience flying. They didn't realize you should arrive with plenty of time to get through security. They walk right past the sign stating that a family-sized bottle of shampoo can't go in your carry-on, that your shoes have to be taken off, or that that big ol' *metal* belt buckle will never pass through a *metal* detector! Don't get me started on the things I have seen people do and not do at airports.

Yet with all the personal challenges, if someone turns to me and says, "I'm never traveling again! This is too difficult!" I will encourage that person to not let any of the hassles *of* traveling stop them *from* traveling. Why? From my knowledge and experience after many years, I've discovered that once you arrive at your destination, it will be worth the hassles and problems you faced during the process.

The same is true when it comes to something far more important: sharing Jesus. Regardless of where the person takes your conversation, the destination will always be worth the journey.

When it comes to sharing your faith with others, you may have tried it before and felt like you were driving on a trip with no map to lead the way. You may be intimidated by the thought of talking with someone about their relationship with the Lord. Or you might simply feel like your life is in no way an example to others. Well, let's see if we can get over those hurdles and any others you may have felt. I promise it will not only give you a purpose in your life, but it will be worth the journey to give someone else that same purpose, and the best part—freedom in Jesus Christ.

Here's an important question: if someone tells you that he or she has a relationship with Jesus but cannot explain how to come to faith, isn't that a bit puzzling to you? I know it is for me. Somehow, some way, we have not done the best job at preparing believers for sharing their faith with the people around them. Christians can give so many reasons why they don't, offering excuses like

- "I thought that was the pastor's job."
- "I don't know the Bible well enough."
- "It's just not my gift."
- "It makes me uncomfortable."

The list goes on and on for why people don't and won't share.

Believers in Jesus need to be prepared to explain their faith and the reason for how they live. Moving forward, I want to give you a whole list of reasons why you *should* share. Just like with inexperienced travelers,

I want to tell you to not quit. Don't give up. Just start learning. Continue with me as we make this experience not just easier but something that can be fun and exciting as well.

Chapter 2

CONFIDENCE TO START

THE STARTING POINT

When I'm in a discussion with other believers about sharing Jesus, I often hear that one of the main reasons they don't speak up is simply that they don't know where to start. People have said to me, "Sure, I could tell someone what I've heard, felt, or believe, but what if they ask questions?" If they feel they don't know the right answers or how to find them in the Bible, many folks will rarely bring up faith in conversations.

As a follower of Jesus, just like when I travel, I like being prepared and ready when I have an opportunity to explain the hope I have in Him. So I'm going to share some of the Bible passages I use when explaining the Good News or Gospel of Jesus. Trust me, you don't have to be a Bible scholar. I'm certainly not. That said, loving to read and study the Word certainly helps you when reaching people. The Bible is full of stories about conversations between people. Showing folks the Bible will introduce and connect them to God's Word so they can start using it as their guide for life.

Usually before I start reading stories from the Bible to someone, I want to hear the person's story. It's easy to relate to someone's story because we all have one. I have found that to be the best starting place. Swapping stories is not some weird, religious moment because we already share our stories every day whenever and wherever people come into contact with one another.

When you become mission-minded with directives from Jesus—the One you live for—you want *your* story to lead to *His* story.

LEARNING SOMEONE'S STORY

What's your motive for listening to someone? Hopefully it's because you care about the person, the same way Jesus cared about others. (Remember Jesus with Zacchaeus?) He came to seek and save. Caring is where that journey begins. When we stop caring about people, or only care about certain folks, we lose touch with the message of Jesus. On the day our lives finally come to an end, it will be the people we touch and have connection with that means the most. That truth is often revealed when attending someone's funeral service. What is said, what is not said, and who comes to grieve and pay respects are all telling of the kind of life a person lived.

We all have a story of our own journey through this life. Some life stories are great, others not so much. Yours may be wonderful and interesting, or it may be sad with lots of damage or bad decisions. Maybe it's some of both. Yet you will never get to know other people's stories until you ask.

For that reason, asking questions is the basic level of where to start in sharing your faith. Simple questions like, "Where are you from?" or "Do you have a family?" or "What do you do for a living?" are some of the most common questions we all ask to start a conversation with someone new. I find that asking questions is actually very easy. Hopefully as you begin to seek, truth can be found. Just as 1 Peter 3:15 says, this is where our preparation comes to help us "give an answer to everyone who asks you to give the reason for the hope that you have." This approach is what separates the mild and mundane conversation from the Gospel-minded mission that Jesus came to bring us.

As you hear a person share their pain, damage, baggage, confusion, heartache, anxiety, or curiosity, the conversation can often lead to deeper questions, such as

- How satisfied are you with how your life is going?
- What questions do you have about what life is all about?
- What, if anything, do you think is beyond this life?
- What sort of religious experiences have you had?
- How well do you understand the Bible?

But we have to be prepared for some of the answers we may get. Let's look at another important question:

- Do you have any sort of relationship with Jesus Christ?

This is a basic question to ask, because the answer is very simple and there are just three possibilities:

1. Yes.
2. No.
3. I'm not sure.

Let's walk through these one at a time.

A yes answer may or may not be true. That could mean a thriving relationship that guides their every move in life. But have you ever thought you were in a great relationship with someone, only to find out from the other person that you were way off? I know I have.

A no answer makes it obvious that they do not have a relationship with the Lord. The hope from there is to find out what it would look like for that relationship to begin. There is nothing wrong with an honest answer. Maybe the person has never been shown what that relationship even looks like. Maybe he or she doesn't see any advantage in a life spent believing in God. They may question if there even is a God.

Many people simply answer with, "I'm not sure if I have a relationship with the Lord." From my experience, this is one of the most common situations. There can be several reasons for this, such as

- a handed-down religion with expectations that have to be followed,
- a past commitment made that has long been forgotten or never kept,
- a complete lack of understanding as to what exactly a relationship with the Lord means, and

- a lifestyle that looks completely different from one that resembles a committed relationship with Jesus.

As I have talked with many people about Jesus, starting when I was just a kid, these four reasons have come up often when I talk through someone's story. While this list covers most possibilities, there may be other factors that could lead someone to not be sure.

So, if we are trying to figure out if someone has a relationship with the Lord, then we need to know how that relationship works. Let's start by looking at how our relationships with people are formed and how they can become great. How do they work? What makes them good or not so good?

Chapter 3

CONFIDENCE TO CHALLENGE

FAITH IN RELATIONSHIPS

Marriage is the ultimate human relationship. Whether you are married or not, it can shed some light into how our relationship with God should work. The point of marriage is a man and woman committing their lives to one another regardless of the challenges that may come and refusing to separate. This idea holds the key to what an intimate relationship with Jesus looks like.

Paul gave us this comparison.

"For this reason a man will leave his father and mother and be united to his wife, and the two will become one flesh." This is a profound mystery—but I am talking about Christ and the church. (Ephesians 5:31–32)

One of the first things we learn in forming relationships is that they require faith. The deeper the relationship you desire, the more faith is needed. But what exactly is faith? A simple check of Webster's dictionary gives us words and phrases like *loyalty, allegiance, trust, conviction,* and *firm belief.*[1] Faith is having complete trust and confidence in someone.

Hopefully many of us learn this concept from the relationships we experience with our parents. Even before we can remember, we trusted them for our very lives. The only reason we survived childhood is because our parents or guardians took care of us. The Bible says something very similar.

Now faith is confidence in what we hope for and assurance about what we do not see. (Hebrews 11:1)

We begin to learn about faith when we're kids in relationships with our companions. We wonder,

---

1. *Merriam-Webster*, s.v. "faith," (*n.*) accessed November 8, 2023, https://www.merriam-webster.com/dictionary/faith.

Is this friend committed to me or not? I'm sure we all have stories where some were and some weren't. These connections and questions continue in life until we ultimately make the decision to choose one person to whom we commit our life—boy meets girl, girl meets boy.

In marriage, we dedicate our lives to that one person, which is a giant expression of faith. We can't visually see the relationship, but we can make it official by buying a ring, having a ceremony, and filing a piece of paper at the courthouse. Couples typically make vows to one another, but after the ceremony, all you have to sustain your marriage from that day on is faith.

Those of us who are married don't carry our legal certificates around with us to prove our commitment. Our rings don't even have to be worn to prove our relationships are valid. Even though the vows we make are hopefully lived out, I'm sure most of us couldn't quote them exactly word for word today. In a room full of scattered married couples, you wouldn't even know who is married to whom.

We all know that any relationship, from casual friends to marriage partners, takes faith to sustain and maintain, as well as grow and deepen.

FAITH IN THE UNSEEN

Discussing faith in relationships is a great transition point in conversations to help people recognize that they do have faith in things they can't see. If they can start to understand the concept of faith in a spouse or friend's commitment, even when they can't be with and see the person, they can also begin to have faith in other things that they can't see. While they may not be able to physically see a relationship, they can still see the results.

In my example of a roomful of couples split apart and scattered throughout a room, after a few conversations with all the people, you could likely begin to match them up. While you wouldn't actually see their marriages, you can begin to see the results of their lives together.

Though I've traveled thousands of times, I still don't understand the many facets of airplanes, but I voluntarily walk on planes all the time and fly high above the earth. I don't even know who is in charge of flying me. I simply choose to trust, which helps me with faith in my relationship with God. I certainly don't understand all the aspects of God, but I have faith in Him.

So, if it's possible to have faith in God, then faith in His Word—the Bible—is the next step.

BELIEF IN GOD'S WORD

Up until the early 1900s, the concept of air travel was unthinkable, unbelievable, and impossible. But once flying became achievable, it eventually led to an even greater achievement in the early 1960s that seemed even more impossible: space travel. For those who have traveled beyond our atmosphere, that involves even *more* faith. I've never done it, but I've certainly seen the results. Traveling in any way above the ground was just the beginning of blowing our minds to what was actually *possible*.

What helps me to have faith in my spiritual life is that the concept of God, Jesus, and the Holy Spirit are very much out of this world, but the people written about in the Bible are very relatable. They are just like us, full of flaws, but very much the same as we are today. They witnessed the activity of God in such a way that they had to let the world know. They wanted everyone that came after them to know about their faith in Him.

Once they showed the world that a relationship with God became achievable, it became believable, which eventually led to a life that, before, had seemed impossible.

> So then faith comes by hearing, and hearing by the word of God. (Romans 10:17 NKJV)

Chapter 4

CONFIDENCE IN CHRIST

BELIEVING IN THE SAVIOR

We can't talk about faith in God without Jesus. He showed up to earth around two thousand years ago and claimed to be the connection to God and the Way to live forever. That's why a relationship with Him is key.

> "You believe in God, believe also in me. I am the way and the truth and the life. No one comes to the Father except through me. If you really know me, you will know my Father as well. From now on, you do know him and have seen him." (John 14:1, 6–7)

Jesus refers to God as the Father, letting people know that His coming to earth was always God's plan for humanity. Jesus is both human and God, or God in human form. That plan required the ultimate sacrifice as Jesus would lay down His life for our wrongdoing—sin, as the Bible calls it. His sacrifice is the source of our hope that set into motion a whole new lifestyle for those who would follow, one of sacrifice for others.

Remember, seeking and saving is what Jesus came to earth to do. The saving is from sins that separate us from God. That's not a crazy, religious concept because every day people are separated from society because of their actions, crimes, or sins. While there are a lot of wrongs that can cause us to be separated from society, *any* sin that violates God's law separates us from His kingdom beyond this earth.

> This righteousness is given through faith in Jesus Christ to all who believe. There is no difference between Jew and Gentile, for all have sinned and fall short of the glory of God, and all are justified freely by his grace through the redemption that came by Christ Jesus. (Romans 3:22–24)

The bad news is we *all* fall into the sin category; the Good News is that Jesus came to save us *all*. He came to seek and save anyone and everyone who will choose Him. His seeking was done through conversations with people to see who would have faith and obedience and allow themselves to be found. The apostle Paul summed up the whole plan like this:

> Now, brothers and sisters, I want to remind you of the gospel I preached to you, which you received and on which you have taken your stand. By this gospel you are saved, if you hold firmly to the word I preached to you. Otherwise, you have believed in vain. For what I received I passed on to you as of first importance: that Christ died for our sins according to the Scriptures, that he was buried, that he was raised on the third day according to the Scriptures. (1 Corinthians 15:1–3)

Paul's reminder lets us know that the Gospel is Jesus' death for our sins, His burial, and His being raised from the dead. He says the Gospel received by us is

- a stand taken,
- the way to save us,
- something we have to hold firmly to, and
- the most important thing in our lives.

We all understand that to have a relationship with someone you have to *know* that person. If you don't really know someone, you simply don't have much of a relationship. But when you do, you believe what the other person says. When you believe what that person says, then you believe in that person. Have you ever said to someone, "You believe me, right?" If the relationship is strong, the answer will likely be, "Of course I do. I've known you for a long time." How that connection happens is belief through knowing.

In the commitment of a healthy and strong marriage, the husband and wife believe each other and believe *in* one another. Usually, where that starts is by saying, "I want to spend the rest of my life with you."

Applying this concept to Jesus, believing *what* He said and believing *in* Him are the first steps in our relationship with Him.

If you declare with your mouth, "Jesus is Lord," and believe in your heart that God raised him from the dead, you will be saved. (Romans 10:9)

FORGIVENESS

The first part of the Gospel is Jesus dying for our sins. We know that when someone makes a huge mistake, a price needs to be paid. That isn't a foreign concept to us.

We all mess up. We break the law. We violate trust. We say awful things. We fall short.

Our whole system is based on making our mistakes right—law enforcement, the courts, bill collectors, marriage counseling, sit-downs with the boss, school principal meetings, and the list goes on. For those mistakes, we pay the price. Sometimes others have to suffer payment too. But when you boil all these down, the end result should be forgiveness.

If there is no forgiveness, we simply would be unable to have any meaningful relationships. Without forgiveness, marriages would break apart, family reunions would be canceled, and friendships would easily crumble. With forgiveness, husbands and wives stay together, family legacies carry on, and friends love and encourage one another through good times and bad.

Jesus offers forgiveness to those who choose to be in a relationship with Him. We are not simply saved or found because He exists. We must decide to be in a relationship with Him. Even though I knew my wife, Korie, well before we were married or even dated, we didn't have a relationship until we made a mutual choice to be together.

In two key scriptures Jesus gives us some insight into who He is and what He offers.

But he continued, "You are from below; I am from above. You are of this world; I am not of this world. I told you that you would die in your sins; if you do not believe that I am he, you will indeed die in your sins." (John 8:23–24)

"For God so loved the world that he gave his one and only Son, that whoever believes in him shall not perish but have eternal life. For God did not send his Son into the world to condemn the world, but to save the world through him." (John 3:16–17)

COMMITMENT TO JESUS

Back when I was a teenager, when a guy and a girl decided to make their relationship official, we called that "going together." I was never sure where exactly we were going, but we were *going* somewhere and now it was *together.* I have no idea what it's called today. Religious or not, we all certainly understand that the commitment of marriage is what makes the relationship official.

When you get married, even though you are two individuals, the Bible says that you become one (Mark 10:7–8, Ephesians 5:31). Your relationship with Christ should be the same way. When you choose to be in this relationship with Jesus, you become *one* with Him.

When a couple gets married, you can see by how they live, speak, and treat one another that they are united. The evidence should be obvious. The real test becomes how the couple lives out the actions to which they committed. It's not just *what* each one said or agreed to do, but *how* that commitment is lived out that is just as vital.

Chapter 5

CONFIDENCE IN THE PROCESS

CHOOSING A SIDE

Getting into a relationship is the easy part, right? Making a relationship great is much harder. It's not just a flippant "Why not?" decision. Someone contemplating spending the rest of his or her life with another wants to know if that person is fully committed. Jesus is no different in His relationship with us. Peter put this level of commitment to Christ in a very blunt way.

> It would be better if they had never known the way to righteousness than to know it and then reject the command they were given to live a holy life. (2 Peter 2:21 NLT)

I have been using Paul's example of being married or single as a comparison to help us understand a commitment to Jesus, but throughout the Bible, there are many terms used to describe the difference between people who have no relationship with the Lord compared to those who do.

- Lost and Found (Luke 15)
- Dead and Alive (Ephesians 2)
- Darkness and Light (1 Thessalonians 5)
- Blind and Sight (Luke 4)

One of the main Bible passages I share when I have conversations about Jesus is from Galatians 5 where Paul describes two sides: those who live for Him and those who don't.

The acts of the flesh are obvious: sexual immorality, impurity and debauchery; idolatry and witchcraft; hatred, discord, jealousy, fits of rage, selfish ambition, dissensions, factions and envy; drunkenness, orgies, and the like. I warn you, as I did before, that those who live like this will not inherit the kingdom of God.

But the fruit of the Spirit is love, joy, peace, forbearance, kindness, goodness, faithfulness, gentleness and self-control. Against such things there is no law. Those who belong to Christ Jesus have crucified the flesh with its passions and desires. (vv. 19–24)

When you share this passage with someone, try to figure out which side best describes their life. Paul starts by saying the bad stuff is obvious. He also says those who *live* like this will not inherit the kingdom of God, not those who *may* have done some of these things. That's great news because we would all likely be condemned!

So, which side—acts of the flesh or the fruit of the Spirit—describes how a person lives? When you ask a person, they will generally be able to identify pretty quickly. If you are in a relationship with Jesus, the question is, do you *live* like you are in a relationship with Him? If not, there's a problem.

THE HOLY SPIRIT

What exactly is this Spirit that produces fruit?

From the verses I shared, this Spirit causes a drastically different way of living one's life. When it is apparent in someone, there is a noticeable distinction that produces all of the godly qualities that most people would want pouring out of their lives. The day two people get married, which list do you think the other would choose as characteristics they would want from their spouse? That seems pretty obvious as well.

In John 14:26 Jesus said the Holy Spirit would come when He left the earth. The Gospels of Matthew, Mark, Luke, and John are where we find the stories of Jesus' life from birth to death to resurrection. In Acts chapter one Jesus ascended into heaven and, in the next chapter, the Holy Spirit showed up big time! Peter got up and spoke to a huge crowd of people to share the Gospel and also let them know this Holy Spirit would live in those who follow Jesus from now on.

> "This man was handed over to you by God's deliberate plan and foreknowledge; and you, with the help of wicked men, put him to death by nailing him to the cross. But God raised him from the dead, freeing him from the agony of death, because it was impossible for death to keep its hold on him...
>
> "Therefore let all Israel be assured of this: God has made this Jesus, whom you crucified, both Lord and Messiah."
>
> When the people heard this, they were cut to the heart and said to Peter and the other apostles, "Brothers, what shall we do?"

Peter replied, "Repent and be baptized, every one of you, in the name of Jesus Christ for the forgiveness of your sins. And you will receive the gift of the Holy Spirit." (Acts 2:23–24, 36–38)

This is a key passage of Scripture giving us the first sermon preached after Jesus left the earth. Sort of a "Now what?" speech. I have always been so interested to know what the disciples told the people who didn't know Jesus about how to have a relationship with Him. One of the key moments is verse 37 when they asked, "What shall we do?" They were "cut to the heart," ready to enter the same relationship with Jesus that they saw and heard from His followers.

Peter was with Jesus during His ministry, and he heard what the Lord said and told people. Now, he was seeking and wanting people to receive salvation. He was well prepared and gave the answer for the hope that he had in Jesus. He told them that Jesus had paid for their sins and mistakes by His sacrifice, considering also that many of them may have been around to have seen Jesus on the cross. He also told them the Holy Spirit was here and could live inside them. Like my earlier flying examples, this was going from the ground straight to space travel, far beyond their imagination! What happened in Acts 2 offered a whole new ball game.

Peter was very clear on what to do. The two terms may be old or religious words for some folks, but two thousand years ago, they sure seemed to understand what they meant. Peter told them to take two actions:

1. Repent
2. Be baptized

REPENTANCE

Repent means to change, to turn toward a different direction. Repent means if you are living like the first list in Galatians 5 of the sinful nature, you must change. This new life will start producing new fruit, the fruit of the Holy Spirit. Repentance is more than just something you say; it's the fruit you will show in how you live.

Several years ago I transplanted a grove of may-haw trees onto my property. They're found in the southeastern United States and produce a small berry. I was brought jelly made from those same trees the year before they were put a hundred yards from my house. I thought I would now have an incredible source of fruit to make jelly for years to come.

The trees were dug out, transported, replanted, and all appeared to survive the relocation. I couldn't wait for the next year to get those berries, make jelly, and then, best of all, eat it. Just one big problem, though. After *seven* years, my trees have never produced any berries. They're mayhaw trees, so they should be producing mayhaw berries. But they're just trees. No fruit. *My trees need to repent! They need to change!*

It's easy to claim something with our words, but our actions will always reveal what we're connected to. Jesus taught in John 15:5, "I am the vine; you are the branches. If you remain in me and I in you, you will bear much fruit; apart from me you can do nothing." If a branch isn't producing the kind of fruit that it should be, then it has somehow lost connection to the vine or the source. God's Spirit will always produce His fruit—all His desirable qualities—in our lives.

Repentance always involves a mindset of starting something new. Yet for something new to come in or begin, other things have to go away. Like starting a diet, there are new items that must be added, while old choices have to disappear for the results to ever become noticeable.

In the Gospels we read about John the Baptist preaching about repentance well before Peter was calling all those people on the day of Pentecost to do the same. John said that the decision to repent was a must to get ready for the coming of the Son of God. God's Spirit living in us goes hand in hand with our ability to change. His Spirit will now guide our actions.

> Then Jesus came from Galilee to the Jordan to be baptized by John. . . . As soon as Jesus was baptized, he went up out of the water. At that moment heaven was opened, and he saw the Spirit of God descending like a dove and alighting on him. And a voice from heaven said, "This is my Son, whom I love; with him I am well pleased." (Matthew 3:13, 16–17)

BAPTISM

In his Acts 2 sermon Peter connected this idea of baptism to repentance. Baptism simply means to dip or plunge in water. John the Baptist had also tied these two actions together in preparation of Jesus' ministry. Now, Peter offered this transformation of becoming something new. He did not give much explanation but encouraged new believers to be baptized after their repentance.

We find this same pattern throughout the book of Acts. A whole new way to show this new life. Paul, who was known as Saul at the time, would get his chance for this baptism. A chance to completely change from being a murderer of Jesus' followers to a new creation in Christ.

After supernaturally seeing Jesus on the road to Damascus, Saul immediately realized that he was actually persecuting the very God he thought he was serving! You can imagine the punishment he thought he was about to face. But Jesus sent a guy named Ananias who placed his hands on Saul and told him how he would receive the Holy Spirit. Repentance had come, so, next, Saul was baptized. Here, these same two ideas came together in a truly remarkable transformation in a man.

Later, Paul would not only preach the Gospel to many other people but would also write a good portion of the New Testament. He would write in his letter to the church in Rome about what it looks like to decide to follow Jesus. Romans chapter 6 starts off with a question that perhaps people were throwing around that he wanted to address. This passage also explains the spiritual aspect of the physical act of baptism.

What shall we say, then? Shall we go on sinning so that grace may increase? By no means! We are those who have died to sin; how can we live in it any longer? Or don't you know that all of us who were baptized into Christ Jesus were baptized into his death? We were therefore buried with him through baptism into death in order that, just as Christ was raised from the dead through the glory of the Father, we too may live a new life. (vv. 1–4)

Just as Jesus died, was buried, and came back from the dead, we imitate Him as we obey the same Gospel. The old is gone, the new has been born. Full of the Spirit of God, we don't keep sinning to get grace, because we died to that life and now have new fruit pouring out of our lives.

NEW SPIRIT-LED LIFE

Paul continually goes back to the Gospel as his starting point, as we read in Romans chapter 8.

Therefore, there is now no condemnation for those who are in Christ Jesus, because through Christ Jesus the law of the Spirit who gives life has set you free from the law of sin and death. For what the law was powerless to do because it was weakened by the flesh, God did by sending his own Son in the likeness of sinful flesh to be a sin offering. (vv. 1–3)

He then lays out another way of showing the difference between the old life versus the new life, how a life with the Holy Spirit looks completely different from those who live without the Spirit of God, or in the flesh, as he calls it.

Those who live according to the flesh have their minds set on what the flesh desires; but those who live in accordance with the Spirit have their minds set on what the Spirit desires. The mind governed by the flesh is death, but the mind governed by the Spirit is life and peace. The mind governed by the flesh is hostile to God; it does not submit to God's law, nor can it do so. Those who are in the realm of the flesh cannot please God. (vv. 5–8)

Next, Paul reminds his readers what it means to have the Spirit of God living within you. You are living in a different realm—the realm of the Spirit! Like he said back in Romans 8:1, once we have the Spirit of God living in us, there is no condemnation for our sin—past, present, or future. We can no longer be condemned to spiritual death. We are made alive! It's the Good News of Jesus Christ that people needed then and still need today!

> You, however, are not in the realm of the flesh but are in the realm of the Spirit, if indeed the Spirit of God lives in you. And if anyone does not have the Spirit of Christ, they do not belong to Christ. (v. 9)

We can get involved with Jesus in seeking and saving the lost by starting conversations to find out if someone is led by the Spirit or by the flesh. Notice Paul says *if* the Spirit of God lives in you and *if* you don't have the Spirit of Christ, you do not belong to Him. Paul does not automatically know and neither do we. So, let's ask! Let's seek and help folks get saved!

LIGHT VS. DARKNESS

One of the last Bible passages I typically read with people who are deciding whether or not to follow Jesus was written by John where he describes "walking in the light." He also gives us some key insight into what happens to our sinfulness after we become a believer. Jesus has not only paid for, but purifies us of our sin after we have declared that we will live for Him.

This is the message we have heard from him and declare to you: God is light; in him there is no darkness at all. If we claim to have fellowship with him and yet walk in the darkness, we lie and do not live out the truth. But if we walk in the light, as he is in the light, we have fellowship with one another, and the blood of Jesus, his Son, purifies us from all sin.

If we claim to be without sin, we deceive ourselves and the truth is not in us. If we confess our sins, he is faithful and just and will forgive us our sins and purify us from all unrighteousness. If we claim we have not sinned, we make him out to be a liar and his word is not in us.

My dear children, I write this to you so that you will not sin. But if anybody does sin, we have an advocate with the Father—Jesus Christ, the Righteous One. He is the atoning sacrifice for our sins, and not only for ours but also for the sins of the whole world. (1 John 1:5–2:2)

Whether your faith journey has just begun or you're ready to start sharing your faith with others, these are some great starting verses to begin learning. Read and memorize all of them that you can. Take the time to read the context before and after these passages to better understand what is being taught. The better you know the Word, the more confident you will become in sharing it with others. Don't rely on pastors or other people to know the Bible. Learn it and live it out yourself!

> We are therefore Christ's ambassadors, as though God were making his appeal through us. We implore you on Christ's behalf: Be reconciled to God. (2 Corinthians 5:20)

Chapter 6

CONFIDENCE IN THE COMMISSION

TELLING OTHERS JESUS IS LORD OF YOUR LIFE

In Romans 10, right after Paul says if you believe and confess with your mouth that Jesus is Lord you will be saved, he writes the following words, coming back to the importance of telling others about the gift we now have in Jesus.

> How, then, can they call on the one they have not believed in? And how can they believe in the one of whom they have not heard? And how can they hear without someone preaching to them? And how can anyone preach unless they

are sent? As it is written: "How beautiful are the feet of those who bring good news!" (vv. 14–15)

While some will outright reject the message, many simply have never heard the Good News. Someone needs to tell them. Why not you?

Becoming a Gospeler, or teller of the Gospel, is for all of us who claim to follow Christ. When we are confident in who we are and Whose we are, the Good News will flow out of us often and with ease. When we are prepared, sharing about Jesus becomes much easier. When we realize that real life change could be just a conversation away for someone, we will

- look for those opportunities;
- make those opportunities; and
- seek them out so that Jesus can save.

Your job is to tell the story, to throw the seeds of the Gospel. God will do the rest. Don't take it personally if someone dismisses or outright rejects you. In Luke 10:16, Jesus even said that if they rejected Him, they're going to reject you also. But that makes those moments when people accept the Gospel that much more powerful.

One of my favorite conversations in the New

Testament is Acts 8:26–40. Philip was a known Gospeler who was traveling around seeking out opportunities to share the Good News of Jesus. Stop and take a moment to read this interaction between Philip and an Ethiopian eunuch.

Notice the confidence Philip had as he shared even though this was a very unique situation with a stranger. He got the message to a person he had never met, from a different country, and was part of that man finding a whole new way to live through Jesus Christ.

A few years ago, I did a little research on Ethiopia. Today, the largest religion there is Christianity, where 63 percent of the 113 million people claim to be believers in Jesus Christ. Doing the math, that is a giant group! I also ran across an article from a 2019 edition of the *Smithsonian* magazine that reported, "In the dusty highlands of northern Ethiopia, a team of archaeologists recently uncovered the oldest known Christian church in sub-Saharan Africa, a find that sheds new light on one of the Old World's most enigmatic kingdoms—and its surprisingly early conversion to Christianity."[1]

---

1. Andrew Lawler, "Church Unearthed in Ethiopia Rewrites the History of Christianity in Africa," *Smithsonian*, December 10, 2019, accessed November 8, 2023, www.

This story in the book of Acts may very well be where it all started for this whole country—by Philip, sent out to share the Gospel. He was led to a guy he had never met who didn't know what he was reading. Philip answered his questions, which changed his life forever and changed the history of millions of others in his home country as is evidenced today.

BECOMING A GOSPELER

One of my favorite stories of someone I had the privilege to share with about how to be a Gospeler is Shellie, a woman around my age. Several times she attended training sessions at our church that I held for people to be prepared to share the Gospel with anyone who was interested after our Sunday services.

Every meeting she would write the whole time, taking notes, but she never said a word. I was told that she had found her faith in the Lord a few years prior. One Sunday morning, I asked Shellie, "Do you ever see yourself presenting the Gospel in this room?"

She quickly fired back, "No way."

I told Shellie that she could indeed share all

smithsonianmag.com/history/church-unearthed-ethiopia
-rewrites-history-christianity-africa-180973740/.

the information she was learning, and the Holy Spirit would fill in the gaps. Little did she know about a month later, her chance would come. On Easter Sunday, our church had multiple services, and I would have to miss one of them to be at another commitment. As with most churches we have more visitors than ever at Easter services. So, I asked Shellie if she could fill in for me during the time I'd be gone. (She confessed to me later that she felt like throwing up when I asked her to present the Gospel to anyone who showed up.)

I came up to the church the night before for a Saturday Easter service and then, afterward, Shellie and I went over everything one last time. The next morning I was at the first service, and no one came in to hear the Gospel. Soon, Shellie came to the room as planned, and I told her I would return in about an hour and a half.

Later, as I was driving back into the church parking lot, I noticed one of our pastors dragging our little baptismal tub out in front of the building. I jumped out of my truck to begin helping him fill it with water.

"So, who's getting baptized?" I asked.

"Oh, a man and his son," he replied.

Surprised and excited, I asked, "Did they come in to hear the Gospel?"

"They did!"

"Did they talk with Shellie?"

"They sure did!"

Shellie had done something she *never* thought she could do.

Shellie had done something she had even told me she would *never* do.

But, on Resurrection Sunday morning, Shellie had a conversation, not just with one but two people, about making their first step toward Jesus. Just a few months before, she never saw herself actually sharing her faith in that way, ever.

Funny thing is, I never had to try to motivate her from that moment on. Shellie was hooked on sharing Jesus. Since that Sunday morning, Shellie has gone on to share with many, many others. Every time, she uses her natural gifts as a mother and her life experiences to reach people. She isn't a Bible scholar, nor has she ever worked for a church. But Shellie has found a powerful mission in life that offers hope to a dark world.

Shellie has become a Gospeler.

SHARING JESUS WITH CONFIDENCE QUICK GUIDE

The visual graphic on the right-facing page offers all the key elements for going through a gospel conversation.

THE LINE OF FAITH—Bold divider from Galatians 5:19-23 centered on "The Gospel."

BELOW THE LINE—Three topics and scriptures explaining the nature and effects of sin.

ABOVE THE LINE—Six topics and scriptures about receiving new life in Christ.

THE GOSPEL CIRCLE—Scriptural foundation for who Jesus is and what He accomplished to provide salvation for us.

Your **COMMON THREAD** will be the conversation, then sharing the scriptures and topics, while a custom version of this graphic will be created by each person's unique story as you connect the gospel through the direction the Spirit leads you.

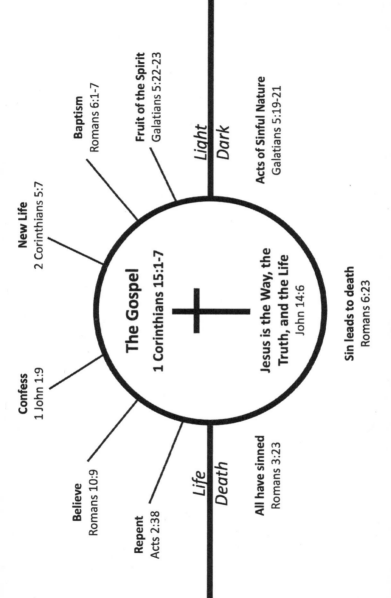

MY CHALLENGE TO YOU

Know Jesus and have your own relationship with Him.

Experience freedom through repentance and baptism.

Fall in love with the Word of God.

Ask bold questions about faith in your
conversations with others.

When others see only the bad in people, look
for the good that could come if they open their
hearts to what Jesus can do in their lives.

Be a person who is led by Jesus and known for spreading
the Good News publicly, privately, personally.

Be a Gospeler.

ABOUT THE AUTHOR

WILLIE ROBERTSON is the CEO of Duck Commander and Buck Commander and star of A&E's *Duck Dynasty*. Robertson has expanded his family companies, from a living room operation to a multimillion-dollar enterprise and destination for all things outdoors. Duck Commander is the bestselling duck call brand in the United States. Duck Commander and Buck Commander are popular trademarks on apparel, hunting gear, food items, and more. Robertson is executive producer of A&E's *Duck Dynasty* and the Outdoor Channel's *Buck Commander*. He is a *New York Times* bestselling author of *The Duck Commander Family: How Faith, Family and Ducks Built a Dynasty* as well as *American Hunter, American Fisherman*, and *American Entrepreneur*. Robertson's story is a remarkable example of entrepreneurship and dedication built on hard work, faith, and family.

Also available wherever books are sold

WILLIE ROBERTSON

New York Times Bestselling Author

GOSPELER

*Turning Darkness into Light
One Conversation at a Time*